The Ladybug

Story and Illustrations by Bob Reese

Dominie Press, Inc.

See, see
the ladybug!

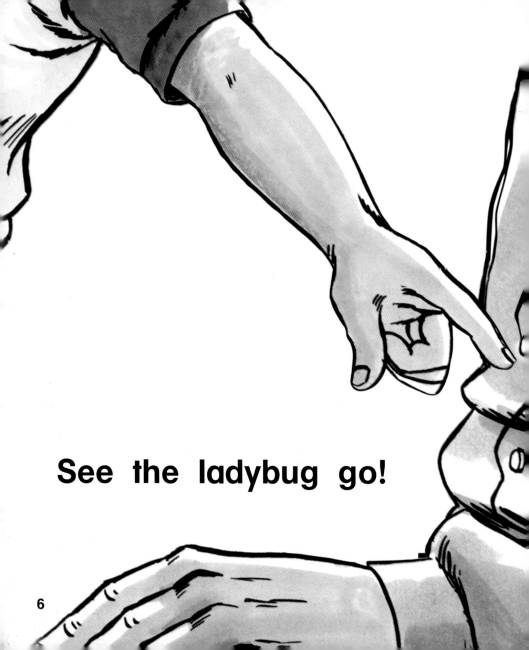

See the ladybug go!

6

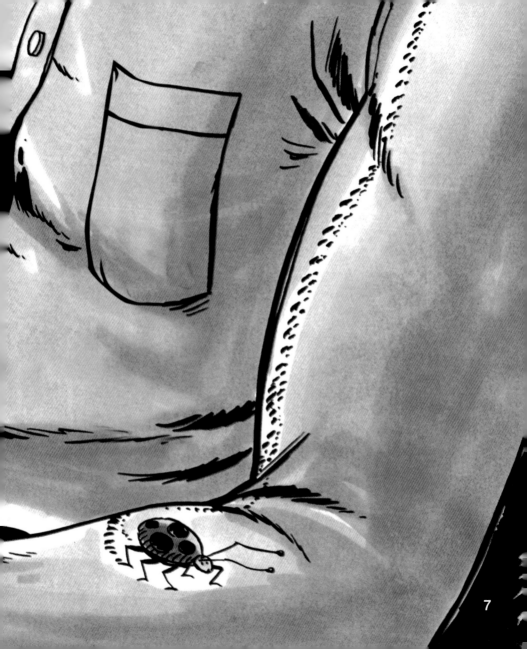

See, see
the ladybug!
Where he goes,
I don't know.

I don't know.

Where did the ladybug go?

I don't know!

I don't know!

Where is the ladybug?

I know!

I know!

19

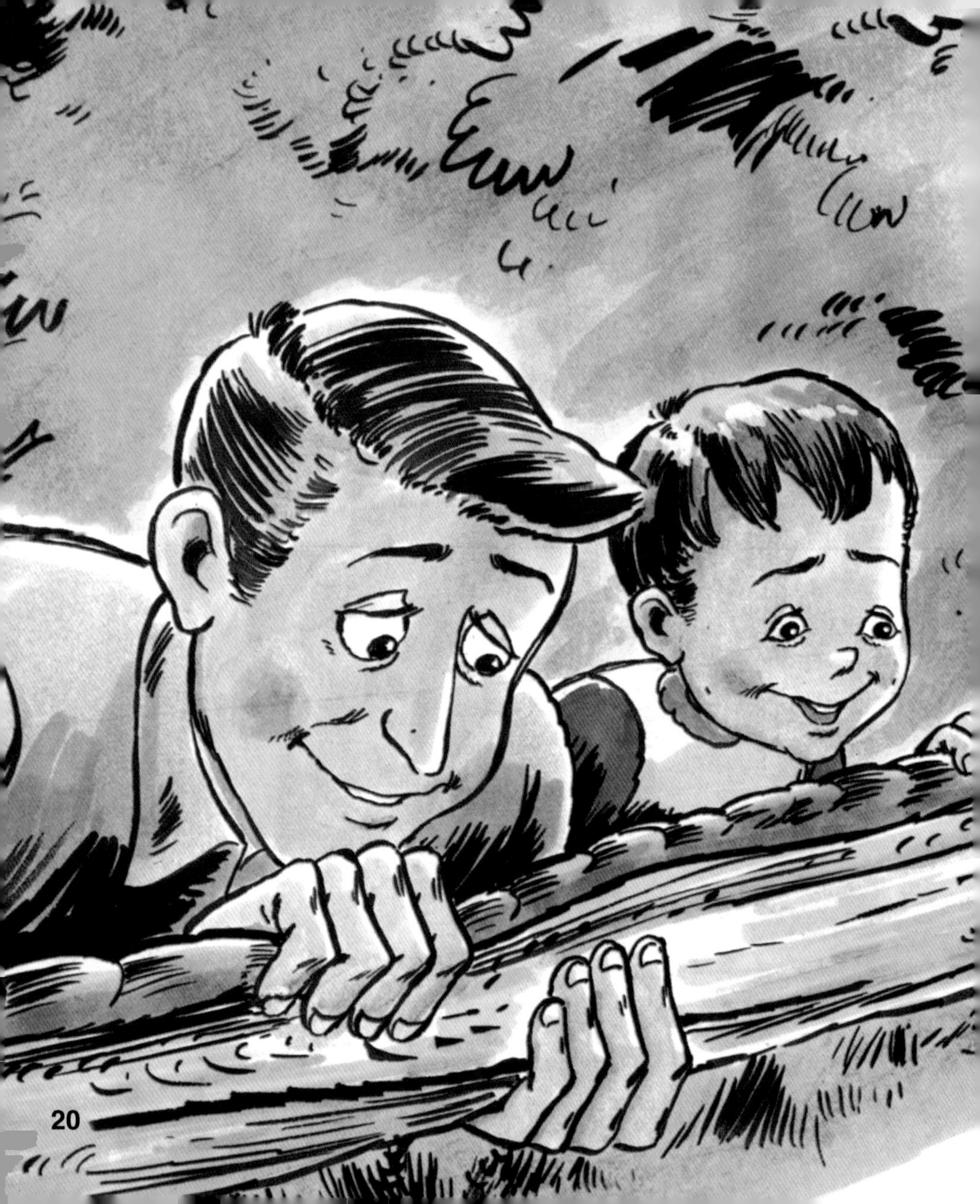

See, see the ladybugs.
See the ladybugs go.

I am a Ten-Word Book

My ten words are:

did (don't)	know
go (goes)	ladybug(s)
he	see
I	the
is	Where

Published by:

🜪 **Dominie Press, Inc.**

1949 Kellogg Avenue
Carlsbad, California 92008 USA
www.dominie.com

ISBN 0-7685-2208-0
Printed in Singapore by PH Productions Pte Ltd
1 2 3 4 5 PH 07 06 05